HUMAN DEVELOPMENT

ELIZABETH SINCLAIR–HOUSE AND ALISON MUIR

OLD AGE

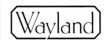

HUMAN DEVELOPMENT
OLD AGE

Adolescence

Adulthood

Childhood

Old Age

Series editor: Catherine Ellis
Series design: Helen White
Series consultant: Dr John Coleman
Picture research: Paul Bennett

First published in 1991 by
Wayland (Publishers) Ltd
61 Western Road, Hove
East Sussex, BN3 1JD, England

British Library Cataloguing in Publication Data
Muir, Alison
  Old Age. -(Human Development)
  1.Old age
  Title II. Sinclair-House, Elizabeth III. Series 305.26

ISBN 1 85210 993 9

Phototypeset by Helen White
Printed in Italy by Rotolito Lombarda
Bound in France by A.G.M.

CONTENTS

iNTRODuCTiON

This woman enjoys her independence, and being boss in her own kitchen.

THE CYCLE of human life runs at different speeds for different people. The passage from birth, through childhood, adulthood and old age, to death is sometimes cut short by a fatal illness or accident, but most people grow old slowly and die.

Most young people cannot imagine ever being ready for death. Throughout history people have been fascinated by the secret of long life. Hundreds of years ago many people believed that it was possible to make an elixir of life – a sort of magic medicine – that would make them live forever. There is, of course, no such elixir. Everyone has to come to terms with their own eventual ageing, but in modern times we are better able to find out what actually causes our bodies to break down, and why this process can't be stopped.

Death is a natural and necessary part of the life cycle of any species, and a necessary part of evolution. Evolution is the development of species of animals and plants. All species are continually reproducing and developing. New generations change, improve and adapt to the changing world. Without new generations there would be no evolution. Death makes room for these new generations. If everything lived forever, the planet would soon be incredibly over-populated.

Ageing and dying may be good for a species, but why do they actually happen? Why is it that at one stage of life we are growing and getting stronger, and then a few decades later our bodies seem to shrink and shrivel and we lose our hair and memories?

One unavoidable change in the body is a slowing down of regeneration (the process of replacing old cells with new ones). When we are young regeneration is very fast and efficient. It keeps our bodies in good condition, helps us to grow and quickly repairs any damage to skin or bones. As people age, the regenerative process slows down until it can no longer keep up with the wear and tear on the body. This causes many physical changes, which vary from individual to individual, such as the appearance of shrinking as the spine compresses, a weakening of the muscles, various organs no longer functioning properly, and a general slowing down.

Nobody really knows why regeneration slows down. One theory is that a kind of waste matter builds up in the cells over our lifetime, rather like pollution, and that this causes the cells to deteriorate gradually.

Life expectancy

If death is inevitable, how long can people hope to live for? Life expectancy is related to several factors, such as genetics (the genes passed on from generation to another), living conditions, and individual characteristics.

Life expectancy around the world

Country	Life expectancy (no. of years)	
	Male	Female
Argentina	65	72
Australia	72	79
Brazil	58	61
Canada	72	79
China	66	69
Egypt	56	58
India	46	45
Japan	74	80
Kenya	51	55
Niger	41	44
UK	71	77
USA	71	78
USSR	64	74

The average life expectancy in rich countries ranges from seventy to eighty years, with women usually living longer than men. In poorer countries, where living conditions and medicine are not as good, life expectancy is much lower.

Life expectancy is also connected to the relationship between brain size, body weight and metabolic rate. Metabolic rate is the rate at which the body works as it digests food, breathes and pumps blood around the body. Creatures with large brains, heavy bodies and slow metabolisms seem to live longer than small animals with fast metabolisms. It seems that small, scurrying animals, whose hearts, lungs and bodies work very quickly, wear themselves out sooner than large animals with very slow heartbeats. An elephant and a mouse both have about the same number of heartbeats in their lives, but a mouse uses its heartbeats in three years, while an elephant lives for around seventy years – about the same length of time as humans.

Ageing can make some things more difficult, but it needn't stop us altogether.

LONGEVITY

In a small mountainous area of Georgia in the USSR, many people live to be over 100 years old. There are stories of men of over 120 years old striding up the hills with ease. How do they do it? Could human life expectancy be doubled? The answer seems to be 'yes'.

Although the slowing down of regeneration is inevitable, it is not this that kills most people. Most people in the West die of heart disease or cancer. One reason why the Georgians live so long may be that they have a very healthy diet, and get lots of exercise in the hills. A good diet and exercise are two of the best ways of protecting your body, especially your heart. Combine these two things with ever-improving medicine, and there seems to be no reason why humans shouldn't lead happy and active lives lasting over a century.

The longer people live, the more we need to understand the physical and psychological facts about old age. The rest of this book is about what it is like to be old, and the many factors that can make it better or worse.

*a*ge*i*ng *a*nd th*e* b*o*dy

AGEING CAN be an unpleasant process for people who worry about their appearance. Our hair loses its colour and may fall out, our skin becomes wrinkled, and our bodies seem to shrivel and shrink. This chapter will look at what causes these signs of ageing.

Greying hair is an obvious sign of ageing. While most men experience thinning hair or balding, women find their facial hair increases.

Hair

Two of the earliest and most obvious signs of ageing in humans are greying hair and balding. Nearly all elderly people have grey, silver or white hair. Some people go completely bald, while many people, particularly men, have thinner hair and bald patches.

Balding and greying affect different people in different ways. Some people start to lose their hair and hair colour when they are still in their teens, while others still have full heads of hair when they are ninety. More men than women go bald, although most women do lose some hair. Some areas of the head may go grey before others, causing a patchy look.

Balding usually starts at the corners of the forehead or at the top of the head. Interestingly, body hair tends to keep its colour far longer than head hair, and may also grow more thickly in old age. This often happens to women after the menopause, when the change in hormone levels may cause facial hair to increase.

Despite the claims of many miracle cures, the causes of greying and balding are still quite mysterious. Hair is produced by follicles, which are part of the skin. As we age, the cells in the follicles stop producing colour in hair. There is almost certainly a strong genetic factor involved. If you have the same kind of hair as one of your older relatives, you will probably go bald or grey in the same way they have.

Opposite: Some people think wrinkles are ugly, while for others they are a sign of wisdom and give a face character and dignity.

Psychological factors can also affect hair. Shocks and stress place a strain on the whole body, and this can speed up the ageing process. A person who suffers a great shock or is under a lot of stress may lose their hair and hair colour. You sometimes hear of people's hair turning white almost overnight after a shock.

SK*i*N

Throughout life, human skin is continually being replaced. Old, dead cells flake off to reveal a new layer of skin. However, as people age their skin gradually loses its elasticity, or stretchiness.

Loss of elasticity is thought to be due to the changing quantities of two proteins in the skin. One of them, elastin, helps make the skin flexible and keeps it stretched taut over our flesh. The other, collagen, forms links between the skin's cells, making them less flexible. As people get older, elastin is lost, and there is an increase in collagen links. The combined effect of these is that the skin becomes looser and stiffer, forming wrinkles.

Can anything be done to prevent wrinkles? People will try almost anything, from beauty creams containing female sex hormones to expensive plastic surgery. Taking good care of the skin by keeping it moist, and eating healthy food will help to slow down the signs of ageing. Some wrinkles are natural and inevitable, however, and they should be seen as giving a face character and dignity. Beauty in an older face depends largely on the attitude of the person behind it.

TEeTH

One of the things commonly associated with old age is the wearing of false teeth. In fact, the teeth are one of the few parts of the body that don't necessarily deteriorate with age. Given the right care and attention, there is no reason why they shouldn't outlast the rest of the body.

SiGHT

It is common for people's eyesight to decline in middle age, but after that it does not usually get much worse in old age.

Many people find that, after the age of forty, they need to wear reading glasses, as the lens in the eye stiffens, making it more difficult to change focus. Also, the pupil in some people's eyes becomes smaller, letting in less light, which impairs vision.

Many people find that their eyesight deteriorates in middle age but then stabilizes by the time they retire.

However, with the right care, technology and medical attention, there is no reason why old people's eyesight should be much worse than when they were young. Not straining your eyes, by always doing work in well-lit rooms, and having them tested regularly to catch any problems will help to prevent damage.

HeaRiNG

You probably know at least one elderly person who can't hear very well. Hearing starts to decline from early childhood onwards — anyone reading this book is probably well past their peak! As we grow older we lose our ability to hear high-pitched notes. This inability to hear high-frequency notes is not usually a problem, however, since most important sounds (such as voices, telephones ringing or traffic) are low frequency.

The natural deterioration of hearing may be combined with damage caused by disease, infection, accidents or too much exposure to loud noise, to cause hearing loss. This need not be too great a problem if the hard of hearing are treated with consideration, and if enough money is spent on treatment. The technology of hearing aids is now advanced enough for many people with hearing loss to lead normal lives. Lip-reading and sign language may also be important for people with hearing problems. If you are talking to someone who is hard of hearing, try to make sure the person can see your lips, and move them clearly. If the person has one affected ear, remember which one it is!

TASTE AND TOUCH

Some older people find that their taste buds lose their sensitivity, so that food does not taste so strong. If they try to make up for the loss of taste by adding too much salt to food this can be bad for them, as salt is known to increase the blood pressure, and thus the risk of a heart attack.

People also seem to become slightly less sensitive to some kinds of physical pain as they get older. An elderly person can wash dishes in water hot enough to hurt a younger person.

Many older people are hard of hearing and would benefit from hearing aids.

BONES AND JOINTS

In old age, the bones become weaker, more fragile and more compact. The spine compresses and the person may appear to shrink. Weak bones can break very easily – some elderly people can fracture a hip with the slightest movement. Once broken, an elderly person's bones take much longer to heal than a young person's. Older women may be affected by the bone disease osteoporosis, which makes the bones brittle. The best way to prevent this is to take in plenty of calcium (from foods such as milk and cheese) throughout your life – not just when you are old.

Old people also tend to develop problems with their joints. By far the most common of these is arthritis, an inflammation of the joints which affects most of the elderly as well as some younger people.

Severe arthritis can make even simple tasks such as drinking difficult and painful.

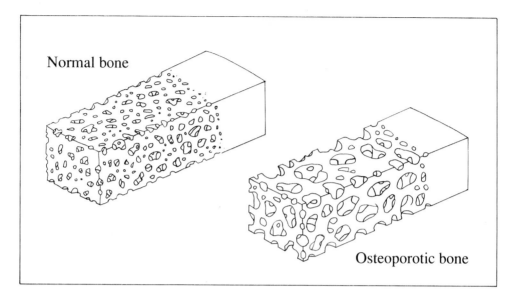

Normal bone

Osteoporotic bone

Arthritis can be terribly frustrating, since it makes movement painful and may prevent people from being as active as they would like to be. Unfortunately there is no proven cure for the disease, and many sufferers rely on pain-killers or operations. However, alternative medicine suggests that massage and herbal remedies, such as eating celery seeds, can help.

Osteoporosis causes a reduction in the quantity and quality of bone.

THe HeaRT

A healthy heart is crucial for a long life. The bad news is that one in three people in the West die of heart disease – it is the largest single cause of death. The good news is that most heart disease is preventable.

There is some unavoidable decline in the heart's power as we age. The heart itself is a large muscle,

This seventy-four-year-old has a healthy heart thanks to exercise and a good diet.

and in time some of this muscle fibre is gradually replaced by a grainy material made of fat and protein. This usually only affects up to 10 per cent of the heart muscle of an eighty-year-old. A healthy eighty-year-old heart should still be in good working order, so that the person can lead a full and active life.

Most kinds of heart disease are caused by the same problem. The heart starts to have difficulty in pumping blood around the body, and if this condition gets worse, sooner or later the heart cannot take the strain and the person is in danger of having a possibly fatal heart attack.

What makes it difficult for the heart to pump the blood? One reason is that the heart itself may be weak. If the heart is not exercised it will lose more than the 10 per cent of its muscle fibre normally lost with age, and it will become quite weak. Inherited disease may also cause weakness of the heart.

Even a strong heart will become strained if the veins and arteries through which blood is pumped are blocked. This is the other major cause of heart disease. If a person's arteries become narrower or blocked, the heart has to work harder to do its job. The narrowing is caused by the build-up of a fatty substance called cholesterol on the walls of the arteries. Eating too many fatty foods such as red meat and butter is the common cause of cholesterol build-up.

As the walls of the arteries thicken and become stiffer, less blood can get through. This condition is

Blood pressure tests help to show whether the heart, veins and arteries are in good condition.

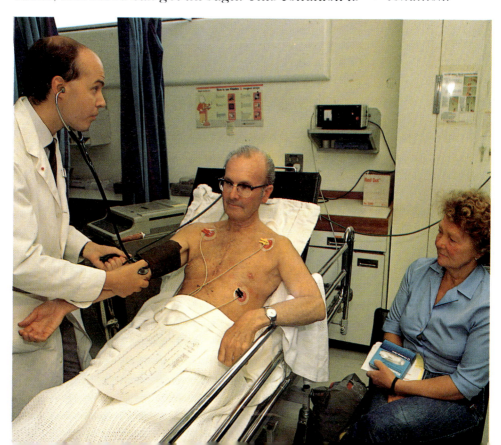

called arteriosclerosis, and many young people already have the beginnings of it. If it gets worse, there is a danger that any extra strain on the heart, such as a shock or trying to run for a bus, will cause a heart attack.

LUNGS, KIDNEYS AND LIVER

There is no reason why the lungs should deteriorate too much with age. Lungs are harmed by the way we live rather than by age. Smokers, people who work in polluted or dusty atmospheres (for example, chalk quarries, coal mines or some factories), and people who live in polluted cities are most likely to suffer from lung damage. Long-term lung damage can cause lung diseases such as cancer or pneumonia, so the risk of these diseases inevitably increases with age.

Exercise helps to increase your lung capacity. See how much farther you can swim underwater after practising. Living in a clean environment is also good for the lungs. Smoking is not only bad for smokers, but for everyone around them who has to breathe in their smoke.

The kidneys and liver should remain fairly healthy in old age, unless they have been mistreated. Poisons like drugs and alcohol can cause permanent damage at any age, although the effects tend to build up and become more serious in old age. Alcohol is not harmful in moderation, but drinking too much can cause kidney failure and cirrhosis (hardening) of the liver. These diseases can be fatal.

Opposite: As you can tell from the clothing in this picture, older people often feel the cold more than children.

aGeiNG aND THe MiND

Opposite: Many old people remain bright, active and independent.

Below: Old age can bring absent mindedness.

WHAT HAPPENS to the human mind over the years? Some people become slow, absent-minded, or forgetful in their old age, and others acquire sharper wits, remembering the events of fifty years ago as though they were yesterday, and freely dispense wisdom to the young. Most of us can think of some elderly people to fit each version. To understand what happens, and why, it is important to know a little about how the brain works.

Without stimulation the branched extensions of a neuron may be progressively lost during ageing.

THE BRAIN IN OLD AGE

The brain is made up of billions of nerve cells called neurons. These neurons are connected to each other and they conduct electricity. They are constantly sending electrochemical impulses (a type of electric message), shooting around the brain from one neuron to another, in complicated patterns. This is what is happening when we use our brains to think, remember or even dream.

One way to think of the mass of neurons in the brain is to imagine a huge forest. Each tree represents a single idea or image, and thousands of paths connect up the trees in the forest. In order to think, dream or remember anything, messengers have to run back and forth along the forest paths, connecting the single ideas and images together into whole thoughts and complete pictures.

A good brain needs to work well in several different ways. The impulses from neuron to neuron need to be fast. They need to be accurate, in order to get the right answer at the right time. It is also very important for the neurons to be well connected. Connections are like the paths in the forest. If there are many paths in all directions then a person can come up with interesting and unusual ideas. The size of the forest is also important – it is no good having fast and accurate impulses if there aren't enough trees in your forest in the first place.

As we age, the electrochemical impulses lose their energy, causing all our reactions to slow down. It is as though the messengers in the forest get old and tired. If the impulses become too slow, some thoughts may actually be lost, as the mind moves on to a new subject before the old thought has had time to form.

Accuracy may also suffer in old age. Unless the impulses in the brain are carefully controlled, they may shoot off in 'wrong' patterns and cause us to say and do silly things. In some elderly people, the part of the brain which controls the impulses stops working. They may start to behave strangely, become more difficult to get on with, or start remembering things that never happened. Most old people, however, remain more or less in full control of their thoughts and actions.

'Now what have I forgotten?' Forgetfulness happens to everyone, but old people may experience it more frequently.

The connections in the brain need not diminish with old age. Like the paths through the forest, the way to keep them open is to use them. It is important for older people to stay active after retirement for this reason – anyone whose brain is inactive for a long time will find it difficult to start thinking quickly again. The more connections there are in your brain between different ideas, the easier it will be to remember things. For the old as well as the young, one way to improve your memory is to connect new ideas with as many other established ideas as possible.

The size of the forest should increase with age. As we gather experience and learn new information, more and more trees are planted in the forest. This experience and knowledge is part of the wisdom of the elderly. The problem with knowing so much and having so many memories is that it may become harder to recall everything – there is more to forget. This makes it all the more important for the elderly to use their minds and memories frequently, to keep the pathways open.

MEMORY

One of the most common mental problems of old age is memory loss. There are two kinds of memory – long-term and short-term – and many old people suffer from short-term memory loss. They can remember names and events from fifty years ago with ease, but not what they were saying five minutes ago. This is why old people sometimes repeat themselves during a conversation.

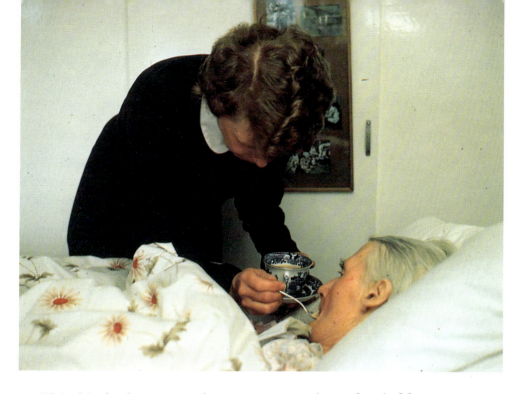

This kind of memory loss may sometimes be caused by the slowing down of nerve messages – they can't store a word or sound quickly enough before it disappears. Alzheimer's disease, which affects the minds of many elderly people, is another cause of memory loss.

WISDOM

So far, we have been concentrating on the decline of the body and the brain. This is a very negative way of looking at old age. This time of life can be one of great strength and growth, particularly in the mind. This growth is perhaps best described by the word wisdom.

Wisdom is more than just being clever. It is a kind of deeper understanding about people and the world that comes from a combination of knowledge

Motor neuron disease happens when the nerves in the brain no longer control the body, leaving the person physically helpless.

and long experience. We accumulate this wisdom as we live, which is why the elderly are usually wiser than the young.

In fast-paced, modern, technological societies, such as Europe and the USA, wisdom is not always

In many cultures, families have great respect for older generations.

valued as it should be. People are often more interested in the latest, up-to-date information than in the wisdom of the elderly. In the Western world, films, television and stereos have tended to replace entertainment through village or family gatherings, in which the elder members would be valued for their years of accumulated knowledge and stories.

The understanding and perspective on life that are achieved with age help people to come to terms with what happens to them. If there was greater respect for the wisdom of old age perhaps we would not be so afraid of growing old, and the lives of the elderly would become more useful and meaningful.

In many cultures, ageing is viewed very differently. The deterioration of the body is accepted as a natural and good part of the life cycle. The mind, meanwhile, is thought to grow with age and the elderly are respected for their wisdom and knowledge, particularly in spiritual matters.

The Akan tribe of Ghana in Africa is typical of many African tribes. They believe that ageing is a natural process in a never ending cycle of birth, life, death and rebirth as a new person. In between death and rebirth, the person joins the spirit world of the ancestors, watching over and protecting the tribe. The elderly are in their last stage of life before becoming ancestors, so they are greatly respected. In turn, the elderly share their wisdom with the young, as the teachers and story tellers of the tribe.

In Islam, the elderly are expected to lead active lives as long as they can. When they can no longer work all day, they should work for part of the day. Their greater wisdom and experience may mean

that this part of the day is more useful than a whole day of work by a younger person. Elderly people are listened to and respected.

Among many native American tribes, the elderly are thought to be closer to the spirit or power that is in all living creatures. They are wiser than the young and have greater powers, such as healing.

All these cultures respect the elderly not just for what they were, but for what they are. This attitude makes it less likely that the elderly will give up on life, letting themselves decline physically and mentally; instead they have purpose, dignity and self-respect.

LiViNG LONGeR

IF SHEPHERDS from Georgia can leap around the hills until they are 120 years old, why can't we? We probably could. This chapter is about ways to keep our minds and bodies working into their second century.

Exercising in old age can be fun, as well as keeping you fit and healthy.

exercise

This man is fitter than most people ever get and is running a marathon.

Exercise makes you feel good. It helps to give you energy, it keeps you fit so that physical activities seem easier and more enjoyable, and it makes you look better, helping you to stay slim and supple. All this in itself is very good for your health, but one of the most important advantages of exercise is that it keeps the heart fit, making it less likely to break down under strain.

What sort of exercise is best for the elderly? Many elderly people have grown unfit after years of

inactivity. They may be overweight or frail. It would be very unwise for these people suddenly to decide to run a marathon. It is important not to over-strain the body before it is used to exercise. At first a person should do some gentle exercise, such as walking, for about half an hour at least three times a week. By building up gradually, an elderly person can become fitter than many teenagers. Albert Rayner became world skipping champion when he was over sixty, and Lucille Thompson was ninety-one when she became a judo black belt!

Diet

Age does not seem to affect the digestive system very much, so the rules for healthy eating for the elderly are much the same as for anyone else. It is important to eat a balanced diet with enough protein, vitamins and minerals and not too much fat. People of all ages should try to avoid eating too many foods high in cholesterol, as these can cause heart disease.

For elderly people who live alone, cooking a balanced meal can seem expensive and too much effort. It is tempting to have bread for breakfast, lunch and supper, without eating many fresh vegetables or enough protein from fish, poultry or meat. More shops and supermarkets do now try to cater for the single person, selling foods that are easy to prepare as well as being healthy. However, these foods tend to be aimed at young, single people and are often very expensive, which makes them beyond the reach of many old people on low incomes.

Just being happy helps you stay healthy. This lady is ninety-three.

eMOTIONAL WELL-BeING

Happiness is one of the main keys to physical health. Someone who is depressed and anxious is more likely to suffer from problems such as ulcers and high blood pressure. Happiness also affects the way people behave. Depression tends to make people lethargic, so that they don't feel like doing anything. They are less likely to exercise, they probably won't eat properly, and they may be careless in the way they do things, which makes them more likely to have accidents.

People who are happy, on the other hand, tend to feel more energetic, and they may live longer simply because they have more to live for. Of course, there is no magic recipe that will automatically make elderly people happier and healthier. However, things like having a nice home, enough money to live on, good company and something interesting to do, all improve people's welfare and make it easier for them to be happy and healthy. By helping to provide good housing and services for the elderly, a country may end up spending less on medicine and care for the elderly.

Living in an old people's home may mean more nutritious food without the bother of cooking.

Life in Old Age

In retirement, older people have time to concentrate on old hobbies and take up new ones.

WE HAVE seen the changes that old age brings to the body and the mind. Now we should look at the ways in which elderly people live their lives.

Between the ages of twenty-five and fifty-five most people in Western societies live with a partner and their children in a family home. They are busy earning a living and caring for their family. By the age of sixty-five, most people are still living with a partner, but have probably retired from full-time work. Their children will probably have left home, and may have children of their own. How do these changes affect people's lives?

WORK AND RETIREMENT

In some societies, especially traditional agricultural communities, the elderly do not retire, but simply stop doing heavy physical work. They may act as advisers and teachers, passing on a lifetime of skills and experience to the young. As they grow old and weak, they are cared for and supported by the community.

In modern, technological societies, retirement is more common, but different people retire at very

As this Tamil woman from Sri Lanka grows old, she will gradually move from working in the rice fields to doing other, less strenuous tasks.

A skilled worker may stay on at his or her job part-time, teach the skill to other people, or keep it up as a hobby.

different times. Judges and politicians often go on working in their old age. Some people continue to work part-time at their old jobs. Others, such as housewives, may not have had paid jobs in the first place. However, for most employed people in Western society, retirement comes as a complete break from their jobs, usually between the ages of fifty-five and seventy.

Retirement should be seen as a reward, although it is sometimes a necessity. For some people the problems of an ageing body and mind begin to interfere with work, or new technology may mean that they no longer have the right skills for the job, and are too old for it to be worth training them. In times of high unemployment, employers often encourage their older employees to retire early, in order to leave room for the young. However, it seems only fair that, after a life-time of work, the elderly are free to do as they please, with enough money to live on.

However, not everyone enjoys retirement. Work has many rewards which may be lost with retirement. It brings a sense of purpose, achievement and identity, as well as status, the company of workmates, financial security and specific job perks. Leaving all this can be difficult. Retired people may feel bored, lonely and useless. On top of this, they probably have less money than before.

It is important for retired people to find new roles to replace the old ones. By the time they retire, many people have accumulated a wealth of

New technology can be as exciting for older people as it is for children.

Being close to children and grandchildren can help older people to stay young at heart.

experience and knowledge about their work. This can sometimes be used if retired people become advisers or consultants for those who replace them at work. It is sometimes possible to continue to work part-time, and some people like to do this as a way of making retirement a more gradual process, as well as a way of earning money. Voluntary work can make older people feel useful and valued. Learning new skills and hobbies is fun and rewarding, as well as being a good way of meeting people and making new friends.

Family Relationships

The relationship between a couple becomes more important in old age. Whereas in their youth they were wrapped up in the concerns of adult life, now they are likely to have much more time together. This can be quite a strain. One or both of them may miss their children or their jobs, and find life more boring without them. They may have grown apart during the adult years and suddenly realize they have little in common. Adjusting to life together is easier if both partners are able to lead active, rewarding lives after retirement, and if they have common interests. They are less likely to feel bored and will have things to talk about and do together.

Some couples' relationships remain strong, or even strengthen, after retirement. In fact, the divorce rate for people over sixty–five is very low. Elderly partners rely on each other more for companionship and care, and most share a very strong bond of loyalty and trust. The early years of retirement can be like a second honeymoon, a chance to do things and go places together. Later, if they become frail and ill, partners can be the best nurses for each other.

The relationship between the elderly and their children also undergoes tremendous changes. By the time parents are sixty–five, their children are probably having children of their own. Being a grandparent can be difficult to adjust to. The older generation has to get used to the idea that their 'babies', are now parents. They may grumble that it

Opposite: As we age, we have fewer older relatives and more younger ones.

Below: Retired couples have more time to spend together.

makes them feel old to be a grandparent, or they may disapprove of the way their grandchildren are being brought up, and be tempted to interfere. They may be hurt if their advice is ignored.

However, being a grandparent can be a fulfilling experience. It can be very comforting to see the family continuing into further generations. Having small children about enables grandparents to relive the days when their own children were young. Once again they can play silly games, tell stories, and act as an ever-loving and patient audience for their grandchildren. Many grandparents are much appreciated by young parents as sources of advice and information and for babysitting.

DEPENDING ON OTHERS

As the elderly become weaker, and sometimes ill, they depend more and more on the help other people can give them. At first, some tasks just become more awkward and tiring – like walking up steep stairs or carrying heavy bags. But life can remain easy and pleasant as long as help is available for certain things. To continue to live active, independent lives, old people have a particular need for certain public services, such as a reliable, cheap public transport system and lifts in public places to help those who can't manage stairs. For people who suffer from arthritis, gadgets (such as electric tin openers) can make everyday life easier to cope with. Friendly neighbours can help in many ways, from carrying shopping up the stairs, to coming round to help with the gardening.

As long as elderly people have a partner, relative or friend to help with difficult jobs, they can usually continue to live independent lives in their own homes. However, if they live alone, or they can no longer look after themselves properly, they may be advised to move from their home to a place where they can be looked after.

There is no real comfort for someone who is missing their home, family and the past.

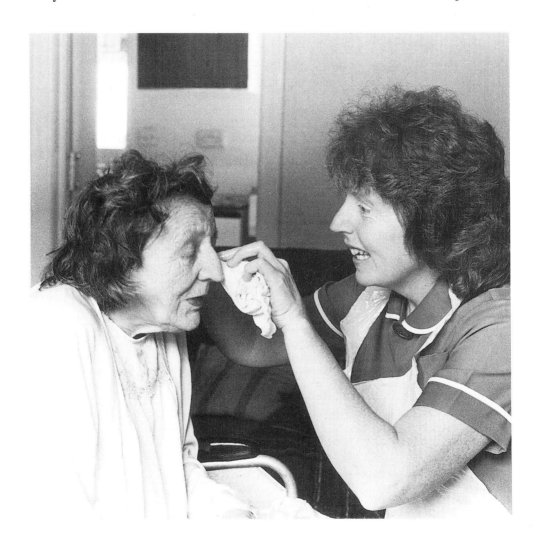

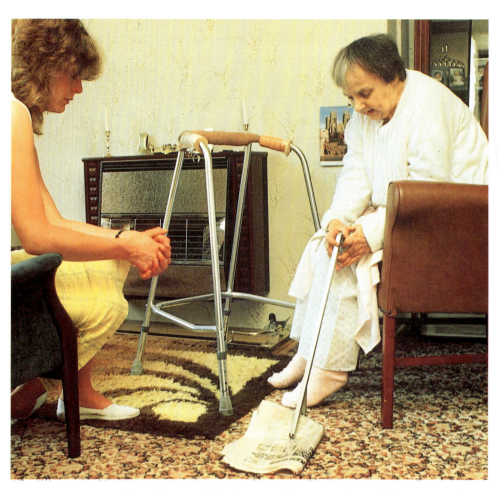

Gadgets like this can make everyday life easier to cope with.

Many elderly people move in with one of their children, and this takes some adjustment for everybody in the house. The family roles are now reversed. Instead of the parent looking after the child, the child is now looking after the parent. Both sides may feel that the other is bossing them around too much, or that they have lost their independence and privacy. There are many positive results too, however. More people in a household can mean more fun for everyone, and learning to live with other people is an important part of life.

For elderly people in need of care who do not have the option of living with their children, there are several alternatives: sheltered housing, old people's homes, nursing homes and, for those who are ill, geriatric wards of hospitals.

In sheltered housing, the residents lead independent lives in their own flats, but some special services are provided. The buildings are designed to be easy to get around, there is usually medical help nearby, and help with chores like shopping for those who need it. In old people's homes, the residents usually have their own room in a large house with shared living and dining rooms. Housework and cooking are done for them, but medical care is limited. Nursing homes are for those who are quite weak and frequently, though not seriously, ill. The home gives them trained medical care without their having to go into hospital. For the seriously ill, the geriatric wards of hospitals provide specialist attention.

Becoming increasingly dependent on other people is difficult to come to terms with. Living in an institution can be very irritating – the rules, restrictions and, perhaps, overcooked food can be difficult to get used to. It can also be lonely, and some people feel as though they have just been put somewhere convenient and forgotten about. At the same time, many old people feel ashamed at not being able to look after themselves any more. They may lose their pride and dignity, and feel that they are a burden to other people.

DEATH AND BEREAVEMENT

This Greek woman is wearing the traditional black dress of a widow as a sign of grief.

DEATH COMES to all living things. It is as frequent and as natural as birth, and yet it is much less understood and accepted.

DᴇᴀTH

Fear of death seems to affect everyone, especially young people. This fear is as natural as death itself. If we were not so afraid of it, we probably wouldn't take care to live as long as we do. If fear of death is too great, however, it can spoil life, especially for those who are elderly or sick and know that they may die soon. Usually old people start to come to terms with death, and some even welcome it.

In Western society people are kept at a distance from death. If someone dies, people are often afraid or embarrassed to talk about it. Children are often protected from it, and it is hidden as much as possible. Death is seen as something to be kept at bay for as long as possible, and medical science is continually developing new drugs and treatments to make us live longer.

Religion helps many people understand, explain and accept death.

Above: Rituals and ceremonies are occasions when the bereaved can show their grief.

Opposite: Losing a lifelong partner is a serious kind of bereavement.

In other cultures, however, death is a far more visible part of life. It is seen as a natural and celebrated part of the life cycle, and people do not struggle against it so much. This kind of attitude makes it easier for those who are close to death to accept it.

Religion helps many people to come to terms with death. Some people believe in reincarnation – that the dead are born again as new beings. Others believe that the dead become ancestors – guardians of the living whose spirits are always present. Many people believe in some kind of after-life, usually in a paradise with a god or gods. All this helps people to accept the idea that death is not an ending, but just

one stage in a longer existence. Even those who don't believe in any kind of after-life may be comforted by a strong belief that they are part of a greater purpose or plan which will continue after they die.

BEREAVEMENT

No matter how well we come to terms with the thought of our own death, one of the hardest things to cope with is the death of someone close to us.

Bereavement is the word used to describe losing someone you love. It is a process of shock, grief and

Opposite: As shock wears off, the real grief begins.

The first stage of bereavement is shock, when the person can hardly believe what has happened.

gradual recovery. Of course this doesn't only happen to the elderly. Bereavement is experienced by people of all ages, and can be particularly hard for children to cope with. The elderly, however, experience it more often, as more of their friends and relatives grow old and die. Bereavement is most difficult for an elderly person who loses a lifelong partner.

Memorials help the living to remember the lives of the dead and come to terms with their deaths.

Bereavement isn't just one kind of feeling – it is a long process, involving several stages and emotions. The unhappiness of bereavement can be

seen as a kind of illness with various symptoms, from which most people gradually recover.

The first reaction on hearing that someone has died will be one of shock. Even if the death was expected and came after a long illness, there will be an automatic, physical reaction of shock. The heart will speed up and the muscles will tense. Normally, this reaction is temporary and will last for only a few minutes, hours or possibly days. If the shock is very great, perhaps because the death was unexpected, it can be more serious and may last longer. The shock of bereavement needs to be treated almost as an illness, especially for old people. Severe shock puts a strain on the heart and prevents the body from being able to digest food and sleep properly. This can lead to other illnesses.

As a person comes out of shock, they will almost certainly go through a phase of denial, when they cannot believe that the death has happened. They may find themselves looking for the dead person in a crowd, or setting a place for them at the table. This reaction is completely natural. The brain is trying to protect itself from the pain of grief by getting used to the death slowly. By not believing it, the person is able to go on with the process of living. Throughout this period of denial there are likely to be sudden, intense flashes of pain as the mind allows itself to understand what has happened.

As the shock and denial wear off, the bereaved person is faced with the pain of grief. There is no way of avoiding this pain, or of speeding it up. Slowly and painfully, the bereaved must come to

It can take a long time to recover from the pain, guilt and anger that bereaved people feel.

terms with the fact that they will never see the dead person again. They may feel terribly lonely, hurt, and angry. They may feel empty and dead inside, as though nothing is worthwhile any more. It may be hard for them to imagine ever being happy again.

As well as feeling depressed, most bereaved people feel guilty. Since the dead person is gone forever, and there is no way of saying sorry, even the tiniest little thing can cause pangs of guilt. An argument, a harsh word, a refusal to get the dead person something he or she wanted – any of these things may be remembered with tremendous remorse. If a person feels too guilty, perhaps feeling that they were responsible for the death in some way, this guilt can become an illness that needs psychiatric treatment.

Along with the guilt often comes anger. The bereaved feel angry with the rest of the world, with God, with doctors or with anyone they feel was responsible for the death. They may even feel angry with the dead person for leaving them behind. This anger may make them feel even guiltier than before. There is no help for this except to understand that anger and guilt are natural reactions which are part of the grieving process. It is far healthier to feel and express them than to try to hide them.

HOW TO HELP

Bereavement is a long, sad, painful process, but there are ways in which the bereaved can be helped.

Practical help is very important, particularly in the first few weeks when bereaved people may need help looking after themselves. Someone who quietly comes in and cooks or cleans takes a burden away from the bereaved and allows them time to come to terms with the death. Money may also be a problem. After a divorce, women are often guaranteed an income similar to their previous income. There is no such guarantee for widows or widowers, and they may find themselves struggling financially at a time when they are least able to cope with stress.

Rituals and ceremonies are important for the bereaved as occasions where they are allowed to show their grief, and where the death is recognized and talked about. Some cultures recognize the importance of these ceremonies and have several, at various intervals after the death. In Trinidad in the West Indies, for example, there is a wake for the dead person immediately after the death, and then ceremonies three months, six months, one year and three years later. These ceremonies are times when other relatives can share the grief, and offer help to the bereaved. The bereaved can use the ceremonies as milestones to see how far they have come.

Religion can be a great help to the bereaved, since it usually offers some idea of what may happen to the dead, and perhaps some hope of meeting them again in another life.

The pain of bereavement can be helped by talking about it, particularly with people who have been through it personally and have got over it. They understand what the bereaved person is going through and at the same time they can offer hope. In many countries special networks have been set up to help bereaved people find someone to whom they can talk.

RECOVERY AND A NEW IDENTITY

As life goes on around them the bereaved will usually begin to recover and search for new roles to fill the gap left by the lost relationship. This can be very hard for elderly people who have lost their partner. They may feel they are too old to adjust to a new kind of life or develop new interests. Hopefully, however, they will be able to fill their life again, perhaps concentrating on their role as a parent or grandparent, or finding a new hobby that brings them new friends.

Life without a partner may be lonelier, but gradually most people adjust to it and fill their lives with other things.

CONCLUSION

What are the best and the worst things about growing old? Let's go back to the body. It is unavoidable that people deteriorate physically with age. However, this decline need not be too great. If people look after their bodies properly through exercise, a balanced diet, and good medical care, they can be fit and well at least into their eighties.

The same goes for the brain. There will probably be some slowing down, but the greater experience and knowledge of the elderly can more than make up for this. As long as the brain is treated well, and used frequently, there is usually no reason for it to deteriorate.

What about happiness? This depends completely on the person and the society he or she lives in. Life is usually more satisfying for those people who are physically comfortable, who have good relationships with friends and family, who feel a sense of achievement for the work they have done or are doing, and who feel included and involved in the society around them.

Some of these things depend on the person concerned. Each person can try to achieve something to be proud of in life. It is also partly up to each individual to try to stay interested and involved in society around them, and not to live completely in the 'good old days' of the past.

Society can do some things to help. The state can make sure that the elderly have enough money to live on and that they receive good medical care.

Organizations such as companies and colleges can set up clubs and courses which give the elderly interesting and constructive things to do with their spare time.

Other help can be given by individual people. Relatives and friends can make sure that elderly people are not lonely. They can also give practical help with difficult or heavy work. If young people spend time with the elderly, this can help keep older people in touch with the modern world. Elderly people who are neglected and isolated will probably fear and dislike anything new, while grandparents who see a lot of their grandchildren will feel more involved in modern life.

In the end, old age is largely a matter of attitude. If the elderly feel happy and positive about their age and stay active in a society which values and respects them, everyone will benefit.

It's never to late to learn a new skill.

GLOSSARY

Alzheimer's disease A disease that causes the brain, and especially the memory, to deteriorate.

Arteriosclerosis The blocking of the arteries by cholesterol.

Arthritis A disease in which the joints swell and are painful.

Bereavement Loss, especially of a relative who has died.

Cholesterol A fatty substance found in animal tissues, thought to cause blocking of the arteries.

Deteriorate To get worse.

Evolution The development and change of species into new species over many generations.

Follicles The small holes beneath the skin that produce hair.

Genetic Something related to the genes. The genes contain information telling the body how to grow and are passed down from parents to children.

Geriatric An elderly person.

High-frequency notes High-pitched notes. Sound is formed by waves of vibrations. When these waves are very close together and moving fast this is called high frequency (or in other words, very often), and this makes a high-pitched note.

Hormones Substances produced in the body which are carried around in the blood and act as signals to other organs, causing them to work in a certain way. For instance, hormones cause body hair to start growing during adolescence.

Longevity Long life.

Low frequency Low-pitched notes. Sound is formed by waves of vibrations. When these waves are not very close together and are moving more slowly this is called low frequency, and this makes a low-pitched note.

Metabolic rate   The rate at which the body works to digest food, circulate blood and breathe.
Neurons   Nerve cells.
Osteoporosis   A bone disease in which the bones become brittle and fragile.
Reincarnation   Rebirth in a new life on earth after death.
Species   The groups that animals and plants are divided into according to their characteristics.

BOOKS TO READ

Conner, Edwina *Old Age in the News* (Wayland, 1983)
Halls, Roger *Let's Discuss Old Age* (Wayland, 1988)
Padoan, Gianni *Remembering Grandad* (Child's Play, 1987)
Van Zwenburg, Fiona *Caring for the Aged* (Franklin Watts, 1989)
Williams, Guinevere and Ross, Julia *When People Die* (Macdonald, 1983)

PICTURE ACKNOWLEDGEMENTS

The publishers should like to thank the following for providing photographs: J. Allan Cash 8, 15, 30, 31, 32, 34, 40, 51, 52, 56; Format 9 (Brenda Prince), 13 (Raissa Page), 20 (Maggie Murray), 28, 53 (Judy Harrison), 59, 61 (Brenda Prince); Sally and Richard Greenhill 4, 16, 22, 25, 27, 35, 36, 38, 39, 44, 45, 46, 49, 54; Hutchison Library 50; Christine Osborne Pictures 10, 23, 37; Sefton cover, 7, 18, 42; Topham Picture Source 19, 43; Wayland Picture Library 48. The artwork on pages 17 and 24 is by Jenny Hughes.

iNDex